ROAD TRIP
1 & 2

LINDA TROTT DICKMAN

RedPenguin
BOOKS

Road Trip I and *Road Trip II, On The Road Again*

Copyright © 2021 by Linda Trott Dickman

All rights reserved

Published by Red Penguin Books

Bellerose Village, New York

Library of Congress Control Number: 2021923847

ISBN

Print 978-1-63777-318-5

Digital 978-1-63777-319-2

CONTENTS

A Song of the Road

O I WILL walk with you, my lad, whichever way you fare,
You'll have me, too, the side o' you, with heart as light as air;
No care for where the road you take's a-leadin' *any*where,–
It can but be a joyful ja'nt whilst *you* journey there.
The road you take's the path o' love, an' that's the bridth o' two–
An' I will walk with you, my lad–O I will walk with you.

> Ho! I will walk with you, my lad,
> Be weather black or blue
> Or roadsides frost or dew, my lad–
> O I will walk with you.

Aye, glad, my lad, I'll walk with you, whatever winds may blow,
Or summer blossoms stay our steps, or blinding drifts of snow;
The way thay you set face an' foot 's the way that I will go,
An' brave I'll be, abreast o' ye, the Saints and Angels know!
With loyal hand in loyal hand, an' one heart made o' two,
Through summer's gold, or winter's cold, It's I will walk
with you.

> Sure, I will walk with you, my lad,
> A love ordains me to,–
> To Heaven's door, an' through, my lad.
> O I will walk with you.

By James Whitcomb Riley

PART I

ROAD TRIP

For the author and finisher of my faith,

the love of my life, our children

and all those road trips that inspired this work.

There…

On and On

The road goes ever on and on
Away from the land where it began
And we are on the road again
Just we two, adventure calls

So many miles already come
So many more before the end
The road it beckons to a place
Out of the clasp of winter's thrall

We sit in prayer within our coach
Praying traditional Tolkien song
Before us Lord, go thou, prepare
The way out there and back again

The way out there and back again,
Tend the paths where we will trod
Let us find no stranger in that place
Through glen and crescent find a friend

Heading south to family
So many faces not yet seen
The welcome we will bring along
Will be returned most heartily

The sun restores the harmony
Melts away the cold and bleak
We note the winged ones on the way
Their flight we echo merrily

Flying South in the Winter

The Meadowlands, New Jersey

Crows smudged the beeches,
sun bathed on the burnished oaks

Geese foraged for golfer's leftovers
dunking their heads tail feathers facing the sun.

Ducks huddled against a fleeting chill.
Seagulls clustered like a chenille bedspread.

First stop, Molly Pitcher Travel Plaza.
Fish sandwiches, a little cold diet coke
I feel warmer already.

The Shadowlands

Locust Grove, Virginia

We came upon a footbridge
out on the battlefield
the fallen leaves were calling
submerged and voices heard

They stared up at the sunlight
from eyes now ever closed
and ground so soaked in bloodshed
rows and rows and rows

The mansion burned so brightly
that day in Wilderness
Men dragged themselves far away
from flames that were expressed

The ground was strewn with knapsacks
cartridges and bread
Muskets found too many marks
too many now lay dead

It was as if they stared e'en now
up through their icy lens
alive once more in homey dreams
happy boys again

As we crossed the footbridge
watching the stream flow o'er
the many leaves, one for each life
implored us, *War no more*

Loretta Lynn's Kitchen

Hurricane Mills, Tennessee

Near four hundred miles from Butcher Holler
We had lunch at the Coal Miner's daughter's
That red cabin in the hills
Gave us an 80's thrill
A lunch stop worthy of every dollar

The waitresses were howdy and how are ya?
I'll be back in a sec to take your orda
Would y'all like something to drink
Have it back here in a wink
I can highly recommend the slaw

The walls they told the story of a songbird
Who rose above, and found a way to be heard
She sang about her folks
The needed money that they coaxed
They worked to raise eight children, love the watchword

The meal was tasty, honest country fixins
Folks was friendly, lots of talk and mixin
Though we never saw Ms. Lynn
Her friendliness within
Will return next we cross the Mason-Dixon

NAS Norman, Oklahoma

Norman, Oklahoma

Old fence
Silently tugging me
Old fence
Circling the air field
Like arms around a loved one

Old fence
Cross hatched small frames
Of their past life
Young couple starting out
Starlings on a mission

Callow young lovers
Yet old friends.
Serving their country
Round each bend

Face pressed up against
Chain link
Stop on a road trip,
An eye wink

Teary eyed traveler
Remembering the time it was
A time of rallying
A time before her existence
A time of off-to-the-save-the-world

It's just an old fence
Circling the air field
Landed so many years ago

Zia Sunrise

Tucumcari, New Mexico

It was that way when we woke up
sixteen panes, rimed
frosty placemats in each frame
icy calligraphy across each page
pink stucco walls gleaming with first light

Sixteen panes, as welcoming as the sign
at the Texas border, "Welcome
to New Mexico, the Land of Enchantment
one for each of the rays
the Zia sun strong
an apt backdrop for our rising.

And Love's Was Right Next Door

Seminole, Oklahoma

It was hunger, and curiosity
drew us through the doors.
And the smell, oh the glorious
wood smoke and ham dressing the ether.

The sign said "Robertson's
Sausage, Ham, Bacon, Real Beef Jerky,
Ham Sandwiches."

What else was on the menu?
Why would anyone stop just
for a ham sandwich?

The aroma intensified.
A joyful greeting
rows of barbeque sauce,
pickled - well everything.

Picnic tables - inside
red and white tablecloths bragged
the usual napkins, salt and pepper.
The meat case was closest
to the register, to the heart,
to the sizzle.

The young man behind the counter
was clearly schooled
in just what made people come through the door,
"Oh, you gotta try a ham sandwich."

And we did.
Two different kinds.
Without condiments.
There was pride and love
in every bite.

Del Prado Cafe

Cuba, New Mexico

For the beautiful Navajo woman in the blue blanket

Anglos. That is what we are called.
We were two of three in the place.
Strangely pleasant to be in the minority
Dine' the language of choice here.

The Navajo locals sat and chatted away.
Del Prado the meeting place,
the adobe walls hemmed in local art
painted spines of animals suspended
swaying in the swoosh of the opening door.

The smells emanating from the kitchen?
Called across centuries,
still satisfying hunger.

Then *they* came in.
He was in weathered denim,
a backwards baseball cap.
He seated her and took off
climbing the step to the other side
greeting his friends
his neighbors,
while she sat,
wrapped in electric blue tradition,
striped in red, yellow,
just like in old pictures.

Her braided hair shining,
tumbled obsidian
gathered where I could not see
Kokopelli dancing just above.

Ghost Ranch

Abiquiu, New Mexico

We were advised to go by another way.
Snaking along mountain roads for hours
in a chromatic khaki
flagged with cattle, goats, dogs,
modest homes,
wee Post Offices.
Arrays of discarded appliances
sitting like strays.

All the time moving
all the time elevating
all the time wondering
would we ever reach the ranch.

A slice of fiery opal blazed.
The blue mesmerizing
unsettling, derailing.
The beauty like sirens in the desert,
distracting eyes from highway.

And all at once, the signature animal skull
the narrow trail of dust leading
now crawling toward our goal.

Rancho de los Brujos,
Ranch of the Witches
Our nostrils filled with the dust of ages,
wranglers, cattle thieves, murderers
and the ghost of a scraggy, persistent tumbleweed of a woman
obsessed with peak and cloud.

Sunset, Earth Vessel

Ghost Ranch, New Mexico

For Camilla

One sat facing the horizon,
waiting, quietly, like a stone.
Do you mind if I sit with you?
I heard no reply,
the second woman sat.

After a few moments, the second moved
inside, all the time watching the setting
sun, while she caressed a mug
gently, as if she were conversing
with its very clay.
She sat, facing out until it was set.

Would you like to sit with us?
I entreated. Her ochre skin, soft
her smile reflecting her recent exposure,
framed in a cocoon
of black and silver shimmer. She moved
to sit with us. The conversation
easy.

We spoke of our travels
she nodded and smiled
adding her knowledge, her
gentle color, personal pieces.
You are in Navajo country.

"My 107-year-old grandmother
left me a string of evenly matched
Moonstones.", and she fingered them
around her neck.

The contrast with the quilted red velvet
a perfect complement to her verve.

Remedio

Ghost Ranch, New Mexico

For Camilla

Soft upon mountains
Gentle on arid land
Seeking healing elements
Woven basket in hand

Mindful of creation
Pruning carefully
Gathering but what is needed
Leaving some for the bees

Boiling, blending, steeping
Wax and herb and lard
Combined in a concoction
For those whose work is hard

Cota, torito and *garra*
Escoba de vibora gleaned
Blended for aching bodies
Bathed in boiled water for tea

Hands lovingly choose them
Planning for years to come
Honoring creation
Honoring God's green thumb

My Father and the Artist

Abiquiu, New Mexico

For Camilla

Georgia O'Keeffe,
relentless to grow grapes
my father told her
it just couldn't happen.
Still she was persistent,
she could not change altitude.
She would not change attitude.

Loving words about her father,
from the indulgent voice of this potter
about a woman whose only softness
lay in the clouds she painted.

Loretto Chapel

Loretto Form
Santa Fe', New Mexico

1. Architects from France commissioned there
2. Antoine Mouly and Projectus. Son
3. After Saint-Chapell in Gothic Style
4. Required were buttresses, spires, stained glass
5. Completed, alas there was no stair
6. Connecting choir loft, and chapel floor

7. Sisters of Loretto needed help
8. Interviews occurred to no avail
9. Gathered, a Novena they began
10. And on the ninth day an answer came

11. A man, a donkey, hand tools, there stood
12. Worked by himself, eight months to install
13. Two turns 'round, a helical ascent
14. Core support accredited to prayer
15. Carpenter then vanished, left no trace

16. Two turns around, no nails, screws, no glue
17. Entirety of its weight, on the base
18. Sure defying laws of gravity
19. Steps, one for each year of Savior's life
20. The nuns now to the loft could ascend
21. To lift voices in praise miracle gained

22. Wood? No local tree could make the claim
23. Rumors that St. Joseph, patron saint
24. Of carpenters, alone the task complete
25. Rumors it was Francois-Jean Rochas
26. Reclusive rancher there in Santa Fe

27. Intriguing chapel found us on line
28. Tree tucked close against the chapel door
29. Rosaries hung high as one could reach
30. Prayers, intentions sent along their way
31. We knelt, lit candles, prayed, lifted eyes.
32. In wonder at the mysterious stair.
33. Stepped away, this poem then a seed.

Relic Road

Winslow, Arizona

Who would have guessed?
Checked into the Travelodge.
Enquired about assuaging our hunger.
Just past a corner in Winslow Arizona
we went to Relic Road.

It was Super Bowl
we entered in,
the Navajo were cheering
offering snacks,
welcoming the stranger
cheering for both teams.

No anger, no rivalry,
just cheering
Their deep brown eyes sparkling
spirited, joyful.
Not one bite of bitter
not one sip of anger
just welcome.

Left before the last quarter
stopped at the door,
joyful invitation to share
salsa and nachos
Won't you stay
Watch them play?

Clearly, we won.

Standin' on a Corner

Winslow, Arizona

It was the next morning
in Winslow Arizona,
we thought we'd go and see
there it was, my Lord, a flatbed Ford
parked where everyone could see.

A stature was a leanin'
against a lamppost
just stiff as he could be
and the flat bed girl, her hair unfurled
stared down for all to see.

It was easy, it was breezy
and then sound of music started
"Take it Easy."

Oh the wise town fathers
of Winslow Arizona.

Leaving Winslow

Winslow, Arizona

Leaving Winslow,
Clouds that looked as if John Ford
Had them specially made for a John Wayne film
Sharply in focus, hanging like a furrowed brow across the skies
Not one blended or fluffy
Proud, chiseled, cheeky, sculpted.

There were not enough hands
Not enough cameras
Not enough shots
To capture these.

Tío Saguaro

Carefree, Arizona

For Uncle Ted

Stand tall * Reach for the sky * Be patient through the dry spells * Conserve your resources * Think long term * Wait for your time to bloom * Stay sharp - Advice from a Saguaro.

At 40, prickly
Actions speak louder
Approach with caution.

At 50, snow-birding to AZ
In Saguaro National Forest
Approach with curiosity.

At 60, revealing humor
Still towering 6 feet plus
Approach with hugs.

At 70, arms reaching
Trips more frequent
Approach with Aunt

At 80, flowers premature
Arms fully extended
Desert harbor to oh so many.

We Answered the Call

Our Lady of Joy-
Carefree Arizona

As the sun, slowly set in the West
hearts, roses, lacey hostess
heralded our arrival.
There was music, a playlist, a player
an American songbook,

Round tables punctuated
in red, white and flowers, ringed the room.
There was little mingling,
same old, same old,
we answered the call
in a new location.

Aromas of antipasto, beckoned
olives, baked brie, salami.
No one wanted to be first on line.
We answered the call.

Friends, family, cliques
exchanged greetings, raised glasses.
There was a playlist, a player
an American songbook.

The props were funny
photo ops funnier
no one wanted to be first on line.
We answered the call.

The music was too loud,
the player was a bargain
the songbook mixed, matched
the playlist fumbled.

The Grand Knight was gracious,
chivalrous, tolerant,
pressed between twin sisters
smiling for the photographer.

The buffet line began,
no one wanted to be first.
We answered the call.

The singer took a break.
The playlist took a rest
the American Songbook held hope
of preservation now.

Dessert, music returned
the dancers persevered
everyone survived.
It was time to go.
We, most definitely
answered the call.

Harold's

The Kiwanis Valentine luncheon
Cave Creek, Arizona

Color scheme red and white
balloons were everywhere
twas the Kiwanis luncheon
just everyone a-flare.

The conventions were adhered to,
the meal opened in prayer,
a pledge, a throng, a sing along
patriots gathered there.

Champagne at every table
smattering of sweet treats
red and white and able
meal selections, *tout de suite.*

The funny doc then took the stage
patchwork, gaudy slacks
jokes older than everyone
earned a modest laugh.

Some finished their entrees
others let a bite
still others finished bottles
no drop was left in sight.

Festivities concluded
one collected all
the candy he could gather
"my grandkids" was the call.

All Ted did with caring
a heart so full of pride
that he had his family
sitting by his side.

Colander Girls

Carefree, Arizona

For my daughters Theresa and Joanna

Old and aluminum,
propped up on a trinity of curls,
punched through with heart patterns
that will never know your touch again.

The strands of #9
thrown in just to check,
then in for two more minutes
always, two more minutes.

I ladle in a little sauce, a little parmesan
strain the finally finished pasta.
A little more sauce, a little more cheese
composed in a pasta dish made in Italy
served on your sea blue Italian plates.

The water boils, I see young Teresa
learning to form pasta, flour in a loose
hollow volcano
filled with the sun,
worked by hand
sliced, dried out on the back porch

The steam rises from the draining pasta,
I see Josephine who looked on,
but was never taught.

Joanie soaked it all up
always added something extra
improved it with every attempt
until finally, she *was* the standard.
I add the sauce to the dish.

Steam rises once more.
The aroma, heavenly.
Theresa who calls for the linguine
and clam sauce recipe, *my* signature,
she wants to serve it in Seattle.
Joanna bears the recipe to Dave,
so he can adlib in Babylon.

All these things, as I strain the pasta
through the heart shaped holes.

And Back Again

Stones, Rocks, Boulders

Dragoon, Arizona

All across the painted desert
Commanding attention
Imposing themselves
Across our path, crouching o'er the roads
Grouping together in response
To earth's deep rumblings,
The stones called.

Shattered into parking lot trim
Splintered, cut for wearing
Cut, polished, set
On mantles, entryways, fingers
The rocks informed our travel.

Large formations, sculptures really
Inciting imagination, calling back
To the territories of those chiefs
Feathered, painted and horsed
The boulders mark arid dominions
Real and imagined.

Another wall fell,
Lying in cultured contrast
To the new, bulging
With folded prayer, rocking intentions
Stones together, still informing

This life long learner
Facing her own falling walls.
Sealing boulders,
Jarring endings.
Who knows that
The stone that was rolled away
Set her free.

The Dust Storm That Never Was

West Texas

1. Zero visibility possible.
I've heard of this.
2. Dust storms may exist next 10 miles
Have you ever been in a dust storm?
3. In a dust storm
When?
4. Pull off roadway
1965? What was the family car?
5. Turn vehicle off
1960 Econoline van with a white top, red bottom?
6. Feet off brakes
Why take your feet off the brakes? The dust gets in?
7. Stay buckled
The dust scoured the paint off? The repair?
No more red and white?
Maroon?
I'm parched.

Uncles Store

City of Balmorhea,
Oasis of West Texas

It seems we missed the oasis part
I thought it was named for an Irish dreamer
Turns out it was three "land promoters."
Turning off route 10, we hoped
For more than a ghost town.

Dusty, dry, lifeless approach
We were hungry,
Coached by our kidneys to land.
Uncles promised to meet all our needs;
Fuel, food, relief.
The plump proprietor, pleasant enough.
Strange noise tics from behind the counter.
Evidence of a deeper concern.

I don't know why I kept the small apple
From the box lunch.
It was small, like the town,
It was good emergency food
It sits on the microwave,
puckering, smaller,
making no sound at all.

Azog, the Defiler

or "Cool Rock!"
Junction, Texas

It was a rocky walk around
the back of the Econo-lodge
a view of the Llano River,
one of the many bridges that crossed.
A story of a *terrible* flood

After photos, my eye fell on a stone
a large conglomerate,
something out of Middle Earth; Azog's skull
lying there, part of the rocky landscape
behind the motel.
There were gaping holes where eyes
might have been.

Just as the holes on the river
where *Above and Beyond* Trailer Park had once
perched, washed out.

It took four of the residents
carried a woman over 20 miles downstream
to emerge unscathed from the deluge.

Azog still thrived, among the ruins,
the silty detria along the banks of the Llano
casting his empty eyes once more
impaled on the bank.

Wee Doggies!

Marquez, Texas

Oh, not far from the tracks
Parched, hungry, in need
We came upon Marquez, Texas.
Pulled into the Shell to relax.

Refueled, refreshed and sharp-set
Up to the counter we roamed
Y'all should try, the chicken fried steak
We added some soda with foam.

The folks seem to just come and go
Everyone an old friend
This Shell station served as a meeting place.
We were treated like kin to the end.

Our stop lasted only one meal.
We cleaned up our spot and "farewelled"
We'll never forget you, Marquez, Texas
To visit once more we're compelled.

Wee Doggies!

Where the Deer and the Antelope Play

Jacksonville, Texas

Along 79
Oh, the weather was fine
The pecan trees there were not a few
The buffalo roamed
And they were right at home
Oh, that song took on meaning anew.

Driving on the range
Oh, the deer and the antelope played
Unusual birds,
No discouraging words
The clouds, they just billowed all day.

Our home's not on the range
But the words to the song came alive
What joy we expressed
Said good bye to the west
And off toward the east we did drive.

God Willing

Round Rock, Texas

There was Brushy
Sandy
Salty
Rocky
Dry Brushy Creek

In an hour we'd seen
More creeks than we'd
Ever seen in a week
There was Buffalo and Spring
Keech and Mound Prairie

God
was willing and the creeks didn't rise.

On the Site of the Salubria Plantation

Washington, DC

*The entire city was built around the idea that every citizen was
equally important.*
- Scott Berg

Just south of the capitol
down the Potomac,
which harbored slave escapes
to promised freedom
the waters so dark that rainy night.

On the site of the Salubria plantation
on the very site where 14-year-old Judah
was hanged for poisoning
her master's children
with arsenic from his
own medical supplies.
Dr. Bayne then advocated
for slavery's end.

We turned north heading home,
National Harbor shimmered in the evening rain.
Thoughts of families wide-mouthed wonder
at the sight of the Capital,
a-sparkling array of nearly 17 million colors.
This night there was only blue
smudged across the dark waters.

The waters rippled,
the Capital Wheel rotating 1.5 times a minute
each gondola facing north
for an unobstructed view.

We Missed the Snow Storm

Laurel, Maryland

We missed the snow storm
after a wet, disorienting ride
taking refuge in Laurel
a Quality Inn, respite.

We missed the snowstorm
baggage slushed through parking lot
carport, hallway, elevator
finally, rest.

Did we eat? I think so,
I remember the kindness
and the chicken.

There was so much rain,
so much rain
so much rain
a threat of ice

a skilled driver.
We missed the snow storm.

Epilogue

Long Island, New York

1.
All the way back
We hugged the shore
Starved for a glimpse
Atlantic beaches
Salty air made us heady
Are we there yet?
Northward steady
Fugheddaboudit welcome us
Across the bridge once more
Paumanok's crowded paths
Led us to our door.

2.
Oh I would drive with you, my lad, wherever you may go
And I'll drive too, so you may rest, In rain, or sun or snow.
We'll find adventure on the road, wherever we might land
And knowing who we travel for, and just who has made the plan
Up purple headed mountain, across the fields of grain
Where e'er we drive, we will arrive from there, and back again.

ROAD TRIP II, ON THE ROAD AGAIN

For the love of my life.

For our children and theirs.

For all the family road trips.

For all the singing of the Stars and Stripes Forever in the car.

For all the readings of Tolkien books across the country, you and your brother playing all the parts.

For this beautiful country of ours, the USA.

For the One who created it all.

Hot Dog

Parsippany, New Jersey

It was foiled warm,
reminding our palms,
all the way back to the car
what awaited.
A side of salty fries,
mustard, onions,
relished.
Hot Dog!

Popcorn

Belvidere, Illinois
For Rob and Renee'

It wasn't midnight
we weren't in the desert,
it *was* an oasis.
Stradling the Jane Adams Memorial Tollway
offering a number of delights for the eye
and most especially, the nose and mouth,
we could smell it long before we saw
the small booth,
peopled with positive purveyors.
Sold one simple product,
popcorn, in oh so many flavors.
What sold us?
The smiles, the taste, the smell.

Spiritual Gangster

Elyria, Ohio

Crumpled shirt, lying across plastic bands
a pool chair cradling this forgotten adornment.
The front pocket an exclamation "Grateful."
The back a declaration.
Who left this important covering behind?
And where was this being now?
In her prayer closet?
In his vehicle, spreading blessings?
I couldn't leave it behind.

Once home, laundered, worn,
I felt empowered, and realized
the shirt wasn't the source.
Fighting Spirit wars required
a different kind of armor.

Laundered once more,
I sent it on to encourage another
Spiritual Gangster.

Signs and Wonders

Baraboo, Wisconsin

We stopped in front of it.
A milk-chocolate and cream-colored sign, —
boasting of the birth of over one hundred of the greatest.
Between Delavan and Baraboo, this American
cradle of circuses, this fertile crescent
of the Big Top remains.
The Mable Brothers, long gone, the Gollmar brothers,
Ringlings, just behind, followed by PT Barnum.

There was a blind hyena, Gargantua the Great,
landlocked swath of land houses the gold
and silver encrusted, mirrored,
ornately decorated wagons, carriages, cars
from the Trainload of Passion.
The social media of its day, the circus bragged
of new inventions, amazing acts, unusual performers.

Under the big top.
Thousands mesmerized by lions, tigers, elephants;
tempted by the smells of peanuts, popcorn, cotton candy
magical parades, nothing but nonsense clowns,
clad in elegance and privilege, celebrated
by young and old, rich and poor, this attraction
could cast its spell over 15,000 at a time.
all we saw was the sign,
and all we could do was wonder.

My Kingdom For a Cup

Blue Earth, Minnesota

Silos rising like turrets amidst the green.
Miles and miles of stalks, silky hair
waving across the farm kingdoms.
They were in sight of one another
hardly next-door neighbors, more like
subjects of nature, associates
of the Blue Earth River.

In their midst, an oasis;
The Blue Earth Hometown Restaurant
bragged of hometown cookin',
friendly service, neighborly atmosphere.

Amidst the signs of *Oink Oink There,*
Home Sweet Home, America,
was this: *I tried starting a day*
without coffee once, my court date is pending.
Home Sweet Home indeed.

Whitwam's Wigwams

Salem, South Dakota

A challenge came from Ladybird to beautify the land
Whitwam took the challenge home within his gifted hands.
There he soon created, a culture intersect
interlocking spirals, wigwams with respect.
These concrete lodgepole structures wrought with plan and
pride.
Something good upon our land, they overlook the countryside.
They leaned, as if the stakes, in tune with unheard flute and
drum,
were in rapt agreement, turning then as one.
Ward Whitwam's concrete tipis, calling us to harmony still.

The Corn Palace

Mitchell, South Dakota

This town is always listening,
ears in the walls,
corned caricatures,
historical portraits in maize.
Everyone lends theirs.

South Dakota Home Grown the brag
this year, a dozen corny colors the paint.
A cornucopia of kids, the artists,
a harvest of celebrations.

this palace has many recipes.
Success always on the menu
poppin' with good taste.

Calumet Bluff

Chamberlain, South Dakota

A meeting called between explorers
and the Yankton – Sioux.
In the summer of 1804,
high above the Missouri
in a place hard as chalk,
softness was swaddled in the flag
of a new land.

Lewis and Clark in this yellowish red,
brownish white clay witnessed
the dawn of a babe who would grow
to broker peace between nations.

Young *Struck-by-a-Ree* – Yankton Chief.
Relentless peacemaker, medal earner,
tribal pipestone quarries preserved.

Dignity

Chamberlain, South Dakota

> *"My intent is for the sculpture to stand as an enduring symbol of
> our shared belief that all here are sacred and in a sacred place."*
>
> *- Dale Claude Lamphere*

Three faces studied, modeled –
three faces meld
in a statue fraught in peace
a peoples' culture held.

Dignity of Earth and Sky
looks 'cross the Wide Missouri.
Her quilt, a shining tribute
honors her in her glory.

Testament to her people,
capturing hope so light.
Her colors moving with the wind
shimmering through the night.

Breathless in the Badlands

Interior, South Dakota

Road threading through
an ancient landscape,
striation nation
zigs that drop,
zags that butte.
Bighorn travelers picking their way across
a choir of rock crenelated,
serrated pinnacles
walls, washes. Damp
rocky aroma rising,
wildflowers spurting,
purpose pushing through.

Joined by native rhythms
Ghost dancer refuge.
Unlikely stage, aurora borealis
the shimmering headliner.
Sharps, Brule, Chadron forming bands
that make colorful music.
Together, an ancient backdrop
for the elusive haunting
glow of the Northern Lights.

Badlands POV

Interior, South Dakota
From the Bighorn Sheep

We can see you from our perch.
We gather just beyond
still, watching.
You ride the antiqued trails assigned
holding devices that you hide behind.

You fondle the fossils,
share with the rangers
marvel at the ribbons of sediment.
We climb surefooted after a quick
grassy graze.

This day we just stand
watch as you cluster cars
around the curve of the roadway,
stare up at the pastel rainbow of sand
imagine the northern lights dancing in the dark.

Get back in your vehicles
Never truly reaching the places
it brings you.
Never venturing into
the dark depths
the bleached chalky heights.
You leave that to us.

Presidents in the Mist

Keystone, South Dakota

The swirl of road that led us
flirted with it, 32o, 33o, 34o,
caused the driver's eye to dart
gauge, road, rearview
mirror of so-close-to-ice.

Still, we climbed,
through storied streets,
pressed forward on piney paths,
until at last, we reached the dark
recesses of a parking garage.
The chill reaching through
thin soles.

Still, we climbed, up the stair,
across the entryway, through the arches.
We followed the clay bricks
stared through the fog
and then,
looking like the dream it was,
the four, in the mist.

We counted on the kindness
of strangers to record the moment,
there, in the presence
of the handiwork of honor.

Frozen indeed. On the spot.

The Welcome Center

Beulah, Wyoming

Driving there in Beulah land,
there came a need so bold.
No gas stations were visible
the wind was blowing cold.

Finally, we identified
a rest stop, desolate.
Still into the parking lot
we took our chance.

Walking rushing to the door
past a slice of tree.
We saw no light inside the place
oh how we had to pee!

We tried the door, it opened
a light was on inside.
We looked around, heard no sound
proceeded in our stride.

Oh sweet relief! How very kind
that missing stop attendant
who left an open door for us
an entry view resplendent.

The blue stone, layered wall of brick
slab petrified enhanced
a memory of a kindness
that both ways caused a dance.

Crazy Peak

Big Timber, Montana

We sat, behind etched songbirds.
Trains, trucks, tin roofs
forming the frame.

Dressed in purple majesty
a majesty I knew from song only –
now dominating my senses, fills my eyes
stops my breath, starts my tears.

The Country Skillet filled
one hunger, the mountain
creating another.
Crazy Peak.

Galaxy Glories

Missoula, Montana

Way past Crazy Peak
just outside Paradise
we saw them.
Extending their reach beyond their vessel
spangled with stars
painted in purple.

These small trumpet glories
open all day, morning
not a measure.
Our spirits rejoiced
our souls awakened.
We knew You were dancing over us.

The Center of the Universe

Wallace, Idaho

Its argent foundation – legend.
Round and round the interstate exit
catching glimpses under the many over
and underpasses.
Cradled in pines, sustained by mines
this town boasted five banks and more.

Our car, coming to rest on Main Street,
hunger making its voice known.
Blackboard Café calling our name.
Next booth customers from New York,
surprisingly from Long Island
our conversation brief, pleasant.

Then the food, on the beautiful
mismatched china, mismatched silver,
well-matched selections to satisfy.

It wasn't enough.
We walked these streets *made* of silver.
Transported in time, brick buildings
calling us to their windows, wares, wonder.

Then we saw it. A sign.
20 steps to the Center of the Universe
corner of Bank and Sixth.
Looked all ways, careful steps.
I stood. Right there,
humbled by the mountains
the mines, pine tree minions.
A vanity dispensed.

The Columbia

Quincy, Washington
For the Wanapums

From above the Priest Rapids
to Snake River mouth,
these peacemakers prevailed,
welcoming the stranger.

The Columbia carved
a vista of hope.
I could see all those who ever
flowed with the river...
the smell of wet stone,
the language of the petroglyphs.

Characters came alive;
the anguish of battle
the fading of a people
the survival of settlers.
A watery puzzle to cross
breath taken.

Eat Here, No Gas

Red Horse Diner, Ellensburg, Washington

Gas pumps line the store
ads adorn the station
fuel memorabilia
fires the imagination

Signs for tire alignment
the Red Horse flying high.
But alas, there's no gas
there's no gas nearby

Red checkered flags of paper
line the baskets round
Breakfast, lunch and supper
options do abound

Coke ads tin and tinted
signs for Valvoline
motor oil and service
they run a clean machine

Chicken grilled and fried up
smiling servers serve
But no place to top off the tank
the pumps have lost their verve

The juke box always pumpin'
tunes to fuel the soul.
We had our fill, paid the bill
Fill 'er up? the goal.

Misty Mountain

Snoqualmie Mountain, Washington

As we came 'round the curve one rainy morn
a mountain called our focus straight away.
The ring of mist atop her jagged crown
our thirst for Tolkien here was not allayed.

Snoqualmie Mountain hovered in the mist.
This hidden gem, *The Moon,* legend so named
its gifts of tree and fire there procured
our focus there just for a mile did stay.

It colored legend rich both then and now
it called to mind some tales of noble quest
someday we'll climb to reach the hallowed falls
but that day, in the viewing, we were blest.

The roads they traveled ever, ever on
this in our hearts forever and anon.

The Surf Crest

Ocean Shores, Washington

We could hear it:
like an aircraft carrier slapping water,
a freight train dancing in low tide.

We made our way toward the clash
through delicate, ticklish blooms
sashayed through sea grass.
Emerged from the makeshift pathway
to savage driftwood,
nouveau totems.

A majestic expanse of unwelcoming shoreline.
Salt- spray, wet sand, drenched firewood
eviscerated by wind and waves
led us onward.
A parade of ghost crabs,
hatch marked wake.

Toys of Neptune's grandchildren
carelessly left and forgotten
a seaweed doll splayed in the sand.
Fauna leaving their holey calling cards,
sandy *pizzelles* adorned the tideline.

Feathered foam sculptures, bubbled and dried
on this fleeting gallery.
The drift logs, adorned in coquina shells,
barnacled bark
as if their "hair" was beaded by a beach vendor.

The sun made foamy bangles on the beach,
in time to lift our spirits
find *our* totem,
head into town for seafood.

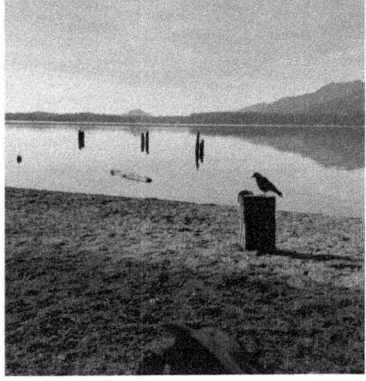

The Conversation

Quinault, Washington

It was no Lake Placid,
but a placid lake.
Ribs of piers rising
peering at themselves in the mirror.

It was a short stub perch,
the crow *not* facing left.
Could you turn please?
I'd like to get a picture.
It was said in a joking manner.
Then he turned to look straight at me.
He had *my* attention now.

I tried again.
Just a little bit more.
Face left. Please?
Now it wasn't so much of a joke
but an experiment.
He turned, faced left.

Now please, hold that pose.
He looked at me,
as if to get approval.
Right there. Perfect.
He stood, as reflective
as the pier stubs.
Perfect indeed.
He never said a word
and I heard it all.

The Loose Kaboose Diner

Seaview, Washington

This car was at the station,
it made tracks to get here, settled in.

Painted in *Here I Am* red,
it called us hungry travelers
to come inside.

Seated amidst
tables papered in news, history,
hopes, dreams dashed.
Sounds of a small train
making rounds and rounds
chugging through the empty private room,
the Ghost Train.

Generous amounts of cash
hung like flags from the slotted ceiling,
the window panes, spotlighted patrons
of a local boys/girls' club.

Aromas of chowder, fried halibut,
fresh brewed coffee,
oh, so comforting. The taste
bearing witness, welcome
on a chilly day along the coast.

Surrounded by trains, toys
toy trains
train toys
A railway of so many memories
to end our travel hunger.

Crossing the Bar

Cape Disappointment, Washington

Life at the edge of a continent,
mossy greens, nurseries, a promontory
of ancient basalt. Misty breath hydrating
Sitka Spruce, slapping the shore in layers.
The understory so much more than brush,
moss, sword fern.

Danger at the Columbia's powerful mouth,
this prickly coast beached and bled the *Vandalia, Merrithew*
the *Mindora* on the Elephant Rocks
in Deadman's Hollow, where the shells of men
washed upon the shore. Snapped,
sprayed, and sank so much hope
making ships into driftwood, trees bowing backward
trying to shrink from its power
becoming a wave of green.

The barque *Oriole,* bearing
the elements of the Lighthouse,
beached, buffeted,
broken in sight
of its future home,
leaving this salty spit of a poem behind.

South of the Tree of Life

Forks, Washington

Just south of the Tree of Life,
drained, bleached, buffed, buffeted
by the wind, water,
lay a root stack.
Topped with
one
lone
crow.
Were you following me?

Olympic National Park

Hoh Rain Forest, Forks, Washington

Your bones, picked clean
by the sea, lying there, bleached
unattended except by the tides.
Called us inland, called us down
winding, wending, watchful trails.

Sitka giants, Sasquatch, Elk buck's
eyes on us, we couldn't decide
where to look, when to look, how to look.
Spike moss, maple, spruce, salmonberry, lichen,
licorice fern, Western hemlock, living greens
abundant, verdant.

The very air thick with the breath
primeval. Nurse logs, wards of their own.
Residents dining on air.

Beneath the footbridge, emeralds, just beyond
reach, shimmering, bejeweling trunks in the sun.

All Along the Hem

Bellingham, Washington

In the state of Washington,
in the city of Bellingham,
the poetry epicenter
of the United States of America,
along her harbored hem,
the following words
floated on lucent waters:

El Shaddai
Explorer
Gryphon
Merlin
Glass Slipper.

Magical names with
masts strung like bows,
accompanying
halyard halleluiahs drifting
o'er us, rippling me with joy.
Speaking to me in
fairy tales, legends.
God Almighty reflecting.

Jewel in the Rough

Urie, Wyoming

We needed was fuel for the vehicle
off Interstate 80, past mini-Badlands
an unadvertised high plateau special,
cavernous beauty, eroding within eye shot.
The road, bridged, occasionally fenced.

We found the station, filled up, returned
to the curved, local route, when we saw
a turquoise jewel, setting prongs – roaming
buffalo, barnboard turned elegant,
cumulus choirs providing
counterpoint in the midday sky.

What we needed was fuel for the vehicle
what we received was balm for the soul.

Buck's Sports Grill

Rawlins, Wyoming
For Jessica

We threaded through the mountains
so hungry, fit to fade.
Checked into our motel room
advice we sought for food

Go to Buck's the answer.
Their burgers can't be beat.
Stomach juices flowing
we were in a burger mood.

The wait was worth it
our waitress was a hoot.
The atmosphere: family party
music, noise, and brew.

She shared with us her story,
she shared how she survived
left behind her silver,
to her own self still true.

The burgers lean, buck naked,
butter key for this lean beef.
The fries, the slaw such compliments.

We savored all, took our time
enjoyed her repartee
asked her name, blessed her toil
tipped in cash, not card.

We threaded out next morning
a blizzard just behind.
Our memory of Buck's Sports Grill
this jewel, the treasure, mined.

The Lincoln Highway

Laramie, Wyoming

There he was, rising above
as he almost always did
overlooking the land he loved.

From *Times Square* to the *Palace
of the Legion of Honor*,
it crossed the country
uniting us in road trip fun
coast to coast,
the first of its kind.

Fisher and Joy's brainchild,
this highway named
for a no-nonsense President,
who was immortalized
because of a poet, on a coin
for the common man.
Sensible cents invested.
Our thoughts riddled with them.

Romano's, La Dolce Vita

Littleton, Colorado

The air was thin but so was Glen.
Approaching cancer by living his life,
loving his lady Phyllis.

He glowed, she twinkled.
Their favorite restaurant
"a family tradition for 50 years,"
our first visit.

Romano's, oh so much older
than their love
no less golden.

They fussed and preened
ordered, toasted with a house red,
lingered over the spaghetti, perfect meatballs.

The warmth they shared
like a precious aroma,
stays with me still.

We Are in Kansas

Visitor's Center, Goodland, Kansas

Poking through with courage,
using my brain, knowing it takes
heart, that I always had the power
I embraced Kansas.

Kansas, where you can see the name
on a water tower for *miles*.
Where vision is unobstructed.
Where Eisenhower grew, along
with Mamie and the sunflowers
in the land of corn.
Where the words drew me back
into the vehicle, where I clicked my heels together.

Ahhhh

Boonville, Missouri

Familiar initials conjuring
visions of waitresses on skates
balancing trays like acrobats,
delivering food and
the friendly foamy frosty mug.
Delightful contents tickling the nose,
Is the root beer icy?
Is the ice root-beery?

I wrote my name
on the mug, the way you do
in a car window from the inside
when moisture gathers.

The experience was a carnival
of flavor, a mad desire to preserve the frost.
A hope for a never-ending bottom
to the logo-angled, wonder mug of fizz.

For the Reycrafts

University City, Missouri

Oh the streets, color strewn
Autumn aglow with Halloween

Our sojourn fermented fellowship
Meals shared, laughs had

Children bouncing in great joy
A welcome found, the halls resound

Music of animated boys, small toys
Memories made

An oasis of faith
There across the wide Missouri.

It Stands

Effingham, Illinois

It stands
vision of John
orchestrated by
Bud who lived
in a steeple's
shadow, something
to make Effingham, Illinois stand out.
A fitting tribute to the good people there.
Moved by faith, inspired by Groom, Texas.
Nearly thwarted, John leaned on his son.
Eight acres given,
shared blueprints
gave rise. Nearly
200 feet reached.
Grounded 22 feet
deep, rebar filled
with concrete
persistence
born.
It stands.

Get Kist

Dayton, Ohio

Oh the Cracker Barrel,
porch always rocking,
shop filled with tempting
tasty treats of memory.
Consistently good food, walls of wonder
filled with kitschy ads from yesteryear
patterned games to count on,
local artifacts, color.
Things that make guests
ask questions of one another.
Endless coffee.
The perfect place
to *Get Kist.*

First Prize – Cheddar's Scratch Kitchen

Triadelphia, West Virginia

The call went out only forty-five days
to decorate orbs in creative ways.

Employees only, Open theme
this contest would be a dream.

Cash or a card the promised prize
inspiration, realized.

We happened in one October day
Cheddar's Scratch Kitchen, Triadelphia way.

So many pumpkins from which to choose
winners all, each one a muse.

I snapped some photos, couldn't pick
which was my favorite? Which one would stick?

The one that won, *my* heart's first prize,
a pumpkin called HOPE, a feast for sore eyes.

Home Again

East Northport, New York

We've traveled near and far my lad,
we've traveled to and fro.
There is no other traveling pal
with which I'd rather go.

With Tolkien as our launching prayer
Tolkien on our return
I look forward to our next stomping ground
and all that we will learn.

Propelled by love and country
and knowing where we live,
to sharing with our countrymen
our adventures to relive.

ABOUT THE AUTHOR

Linda Trott Dickman–an award winning poet, author of four chapbooks. Her work has been featured in local and international anthologies   She is the coordinator of poetry for the Northport Arts Coalition. She teaches at local museums, leads a poetry workshop at Samantha's Li'l Bit O' Heaven coffee house.

ALSO BY LINDA TROTT DICKMAN

Also by Linda Trott Dickman

Robes - The Art of Being Covered

The Air That I Breathe

Road Trip

Road Trip 2

Catching the Light—a book of poetry prompts for children of all ages

www.ingramcontent.com/pod-product-compliance
Lightning Source LLC
Chambersburg PA
CBHW031932090426
42811CB00002B/163